AROUND TOWN

LIBRARY

by Alissa Thielges

shelves

reading corner

Look for these words and pictures as you read.

drop box

computer

Let's go to the library!
What will we see?

Books ONLY
DVDs • CDs
LIBRARY
RETURN
LIBRARY
RETURN

drop box

Look at the drop box.

It opens.

You return books there.

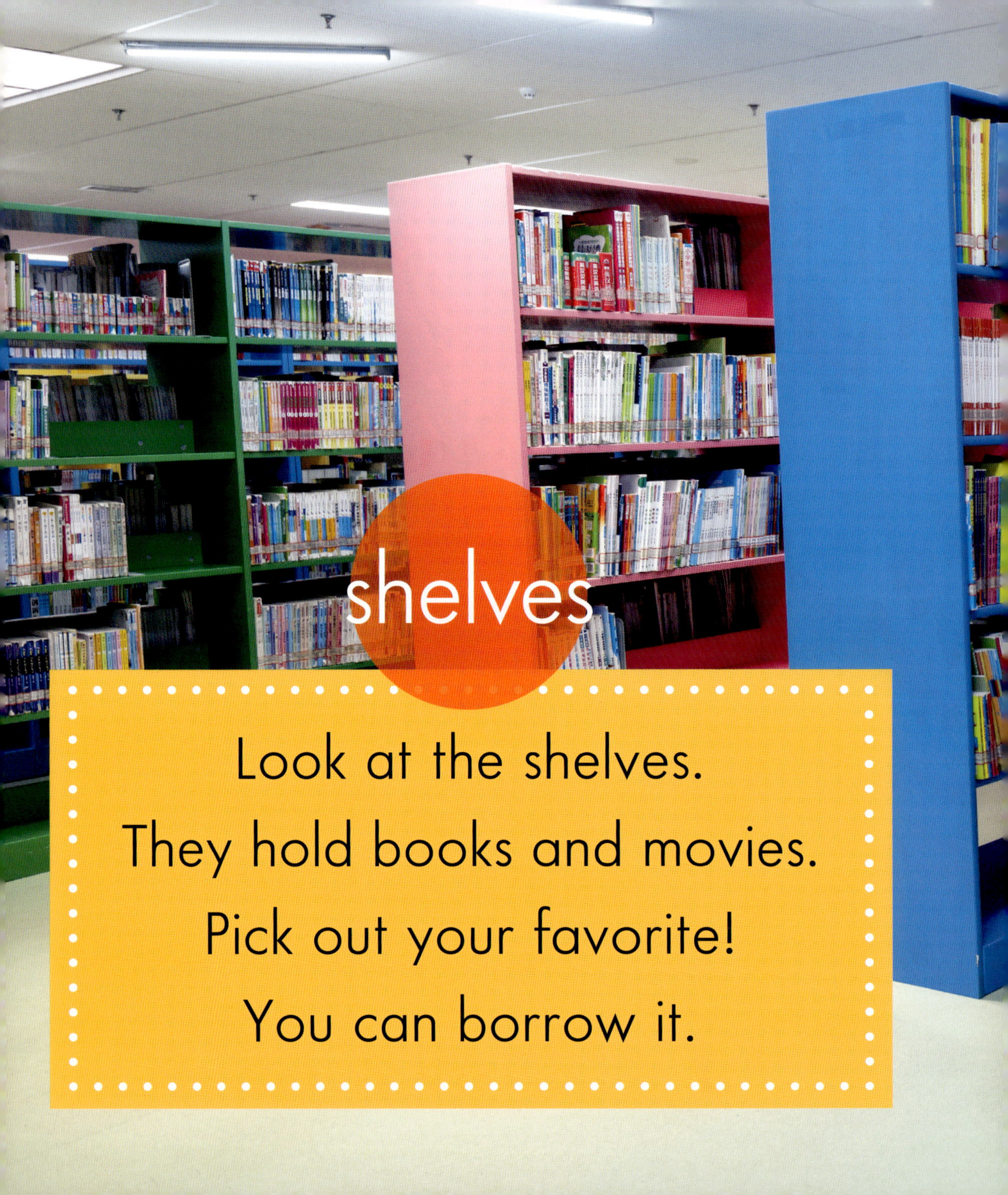

shelves

Look at the shelves.
They hold books and movies.
Pick out your favorite!
You can borrow it.

Librarians work here.
They help find books.
They plan fun events.

computer

Look at the computers.
They are free to use.
You need a library card.

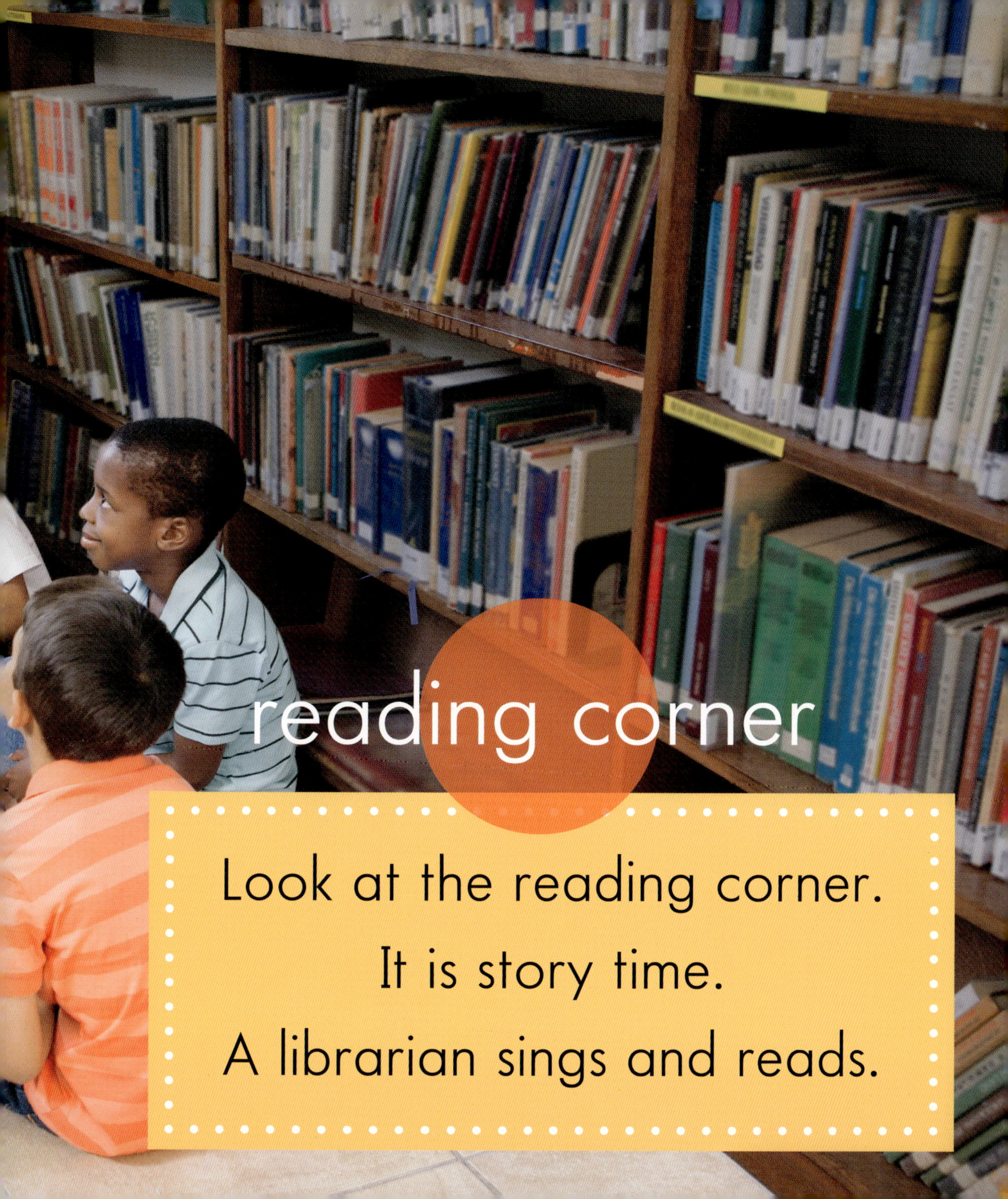

reading corner

Look at the reading corner.
It is story time.
A librarian sings and reads.

Time to check out!
A librarian scans the books.
See you next time!

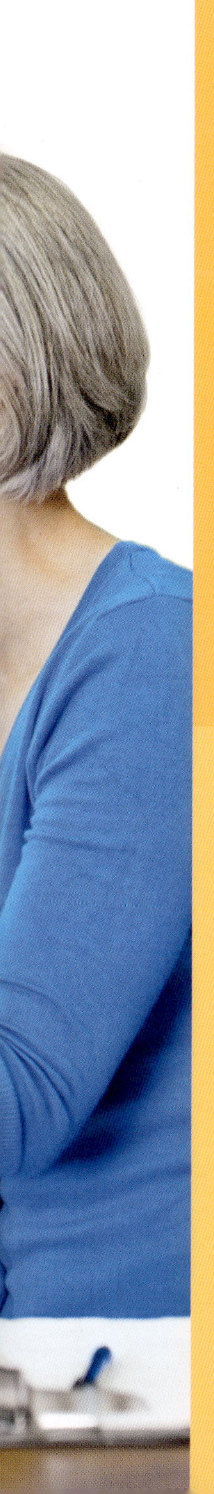

shelves

reading corner

Did you find?

drop box

computer

Spot is published by Amicus Learning, an imprint of Amicus
P.O. Box 227, Mankato, MN 56002
www.amicuspublishing.us

Library of Congress Cataloging-in-Publication Data
Names: Thielges, Alissa, 1995- author.
Title: Library / by Alissa Thielges.
Description: Mankato : Amicus Learning, 2024. | Series: Spot around town | Audience: Ages 4–7. | Audience: Grades K–1. | Summary: "A search-and-find book about libraries reinforces new vocabulary to build reading success while close-up images of places and buildings captivate young audiences. A great early social studies book to inspire learning about communities on field trips for kindergartners and first graders"—Provided by publisher.
Identifiers: LCCN 2023039320 (print) | LCCN 2023039321 (ebook) | ISBN 9781645497349 (library binding) | ISBN 9781645497424 (pdf)
Subjects: LCSH: Libraries—Juvenile literature.
Classification: LCC Z665.5 .T477 2024 (print) | LCC Z665.5 (ebook) | DDC 027—dc23/eng/20231012
LC record available at https://lccn.loc.gov/2023039320
LC ebook record available at https://lccn.loc.gov/2023039321

Printed in China

Rebecca Glaser, editor
Deb Miner, series designer
Kim Pfeffer, book designer and photo researcher

Photos by 123RF/mikdam, cover, wavebreakmediamicro, 12–13; Adobe Stock/ABCDstock, 4–5, JCM, 1; Alamy Stock Photo/William Morgan, 4–5; Dreamstime/Ales Utouka, 10–11; iStock/liu mingzhu, 6–7, RgStudio, 8-9, RiverNorthPhotography, 3, SDI Productions, 14